Fish-it!
Lincolnshire

Follow us on Facebook & Twitter
@ fishitbooks

Published by:
Arc Publishing and Print
166 Knowle Lane
Bents Green
Sheffield
S11 9SJ

Produced By: Chris Keeling

Text copyright 2013 © Chris Keeling
Photographic copyright © Chris Keeling

The rights of Chris Keeling and his work have been asserted by him in
accordance with the
Copyright, Design Patent Act 1988

Whilst every effort has been made to ensure the contents of this
publication are accurate at the time of publishing,
Arc Publishing and Print and those involved in producing the content
of "Fish It!" cannot be held responsible for any errors, omissions or
changes in the details of this guide or for the consequences of any
reliance on the information provided in it. We have tried to ensure
accuracy in this guide but things do change and we would be grateful
if readers could advise us of any inaccuracies they have found.

ISBN:
978-1-906722-29-6

ACKNOWLEDGEMENTS

I would like to thank the following for their
help in producing this guide:

Barbara Clifton and Barry Mallett of the Boston & District Angling Association.

Colin Parker of the Lincoln & District Angling Association.

Thank you to all fishery owners who kindly provided information

and to those that gave permission to use

images from their websites.

I have tried to ensure the accuracy of this guide but things do change
very quickly so if you know of any inaccuracies or any fisheries I have
not included I would be grateful if you could fill out and return the form
at the back of the guide.

June 2013

Arc Publishing and Print
166 Knowle Lane
Bents Green
Sheffield
S11 9SJ

W E L C O M E

Lincolnshire has more fishing ponds and lakes than any other county in the country. This third edition of Fish-it Lincolnshire has many new fisheries for you to try. Some are only a few years old and others are mature waters than I have just discovered. Many of the fisheries are ideal for holidays, with lodges, cottages and caravans available for hire.

Like many other anglers, my time on the bank is limited, but I like to grab a few hours fishing whenever and wherever I can.
Bearing this in mind, I have put together this third edition of 'Fish-it Lincolnshire' with details of some of the best day ticket waters in the area.
Each page has all the details you need to choose a venue that suits your method of fishing. It will give you an idea of what the fishery is like before setting off on a lengthy (and now with petrol prices so high) expensive journey.

Fishing attracts so many people. Perhaps it is the solitude in often beautiful surroundings. Of course there is also the eager anticipation of catching the big one! The bankside can be almost hypnotic and the desire to catch just one more fish has spoilt many a meal.

I hope you find this book useful and wish you good luck, good fishing and remember -
"A bad day's fishing is still better than a good day's work!"

Chris Keeling

C O N T E N T S

ABOUT THIS GUIDE

To help you locate a fishery, the venues have been arranged in alphabetical order and split into three sections, fisheries, rivers and drains. Their approximate location has been indicated on a map on page 7.

Green Section — Fisheries

Blue Section — Rivers

Red Section — Drains

Each page contains details of a fishery, with information on the following:

Ticket Price: All day ticket costs plus details on OAPs, disabled and junior concessions.

Directions: Usually from the nearest city or town, or from the closest motorway junction.

Description: A brief outline of what the fishery looks like plus details on features such as islands, depths and the best places to fish.

Types of Fish: List of species present, many with estimated weights.

Rules/Bans: The restrictions set by the fishery on type of baits, hooks etc.

Number of Lakes: The number of waters available to fish at the venue.

Facilities: What is available at each location i.e. cafe.

Telephone: The number of either the owner, angling club secretary or match organiser.

Sat Nav: Post Codes for use on satellite navigation systems.

S P E C I E S / S Y M B O L S

Fish most commonly found in the Lincolnshire area.

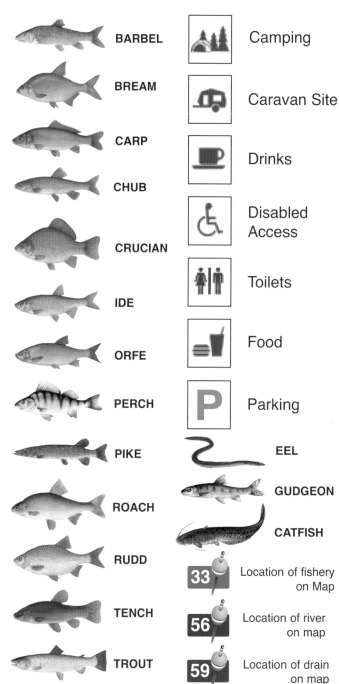

BARBEL	Camping
BREAM	Caravan Site
CARP	Drinks
CHUB	Disabled Access
CRUCIAN	Toilets
IDE	Food
ORFE	Parking
PERCH	EEL
PIKE	GUDGEON
ROACH	CATFISH
RUDD	33 Location of fishery on Map
TENCH	56 Location of river on map
TROUT	59 Location of drain on map

POLE FISHING
FOR THE BEGINNER

Of all the different methods of fishing I've tried, I haven't found any of them as accurate or as easy as pole fishing. To be able to place your bait and feed to the exact spot, sometimes only inches from an island or group of reeds is what makes pole fishing so productive and fun.

TACKLE NEEDED

A Pole

Poles come in various sizes, from 4 metres (usually called a whip) to poles of 18.5 metres. They also vary dramatically in price as well, this is usually governed by weight and rigidity. The lighter and straighter (no droop at the end) the more expensive they are. I recommend a pole between 11 and 13 metres, stay away from the smaller telescopic ones. Many tackle shops have poles ready assembled for you to handle, make sure you are comfortable with its weight and it feels well balanced. Test that it takes apart smoothly. If possible, get a pole with a spare top section as they enable you to rig up for different species and size of fish.

Pole Rigs

Experienced anglers can make up their own pole rigs but beginners are advised to buy ready-made. There are plenty of quality ready made rigs available for as little as £2.99. These rigs come with a main line with a loop on the end (used to attach the line to the stonfo connector at the tip of your pole). A float with enough shot below it to cock it nicely in the water and a length of lower breaking strain line, which has a spade end hook tied to it. The float and shot can slide down the line and be adjusted accordingly.

Pole Elastic

The elastic that runs through the top sections of your pole cushions the fight of a hooked fish and allows you to play it. Elastics are graded in sizes 1-20.
The following list is a good guide for the beginner:
1. For small roach and perch for example - use a No4 elastic with a 1lb hook length and a 2lb main line.
2. If fishing for small carp and tench or skimmer bream use a No8 or 10 elastic with a 3.5lb main line and 2.5lb hook length.
3. When fishing for carp up to 12lbs use a No16 to 18 elastic, and a main line of 8lb with a 6.5lb hook length.

START TO FISH

Fishing Position

Get your seatbox in position. Ideally, when sitting on the box, your thighs should be in a horizontal position, at right angles to your lower leg. Holding the pole correctly makes it comfortable for long periods and prevents backache. For a right handed person you need to rest the pole across your knees with your left hand supporting it. Put your right forearm along the end of the pole and firmly grip the pole with your right hand. Have close to hand - your bait, landing net, disgorger and anything else you may require for your days fishing. It is important to have your pole roller in the correct location. The pole has to be well balanced in your hands when it leaves the roller - this prevents rig tangles when shipping out.

Start Fishing

You have set up your pole and plumbed your depth - so now you are ready to fish. Make sure you have between 10" and 20" of line between the tip and float. In more windy conditions you may want to lengthen this. Feed your swim with groundbait (if allowed) plus a few bits of your hook bait. This is more accurately done using a pole cup which can be fixed to the end of your pole. Put your bait on the hook and ship out your pole trying to keep your rig in the water as this prevents tangles. Lay the rig on the water lengthways. The shot on the line will pull the line under the water and cock the float.
Enjoy your first pole fishing day!

FISHERY LOCATION MAP

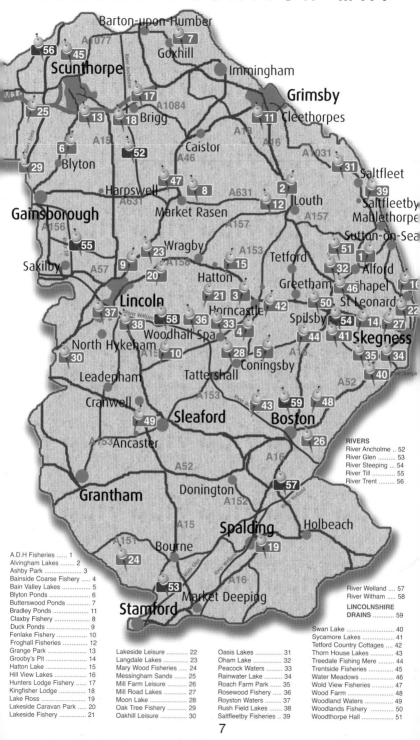

RIVERS
River Ancholme .. 52
River Glen 53
River Steeping ... 54
River Till 55
River Trent 56

River Welland 57
River Witham 58

**LINCOLNSHIRE
DRAINS** 59

A.D.H Fisheries

Stain Lane, Strubby Grange, Strubby, Alford.

SAT LN13 0PF NAV

Ticket Price: The lakes are open from dawn to dusk.
Day tickets are available from the bankside.
Home Lake/Canal Lake - £6 per day or £16 for 24hrs.
Specimen Lake - £15 day (maximum of 3 rods).
£25 for 24hrs (from 9am – 9am)

Directions: From Mablethorpe head towards Alford on the A1104. At Maltby le Marsh turn right. After 2 miles you will reach Strubby. Take Stain Lane. Follow until you reach the fishery.

Description: There are 3 fishing lakes offering a variety of fishing. The lakes have many features, including islands, reeds, lily pads and overhanging trees. The thick trees surrounding the lakes are good for shade or shelter in both summer and winter. There are pegs with good disabled access that you can drive right up to. This is an excellent fishery set in a picturesque rural area.

Types of Fish: Carp up to 40lbs, Bream, Tench, Roach, Rudd and Chubb

Rules/Bans: All fish to be returned to lake. No litter to be left. We prefer you not to use keep nets except for match fishing. Barbless hooks only. De-hooking mats MUST be used when landing fish. 14's and under MUST be accompanied by an adult. No rod to be left unattended. No stalking of fish, you must fish from a peg.

Facilities:

Number of Lakes: Three
Telephone: 01507 450236

Sat Nav: LN13 0PF

There is also a lodge on the Specimen lake which you can rent for £10 extra with a minimum of 24hr booking.

Alvingham Lakes

Lock Road, Alvingham, Louth.

SAT NAV **LN11 7EU**

Ticket Price: Adults £5.00. Seniors £4.00. Juniors £4.00.

Directions: Head out of Louth on the Alvingham Road. Just as you are entering Alvingham turn right on to Lock Road. Turn right just over a small bridge and continue until you see the fishery on your left.

Description: There are two lakes to try. Monkey Lake which has 22 pegs and is around 3 feet deep. It's stocked with common and mirror carp, roach, rudd, tench and bream. Grass Lake has 16 pegs and an average depth of 4-6ft. This lake is stocked with common, mirror, grass and crucian carp, roach, rudd, bream and tench. The largest common to date is 18lb 7oz. Favourite baits are luncheon meat, sweetcorn, maggot, hookable pellets, paste and bread. A loyalty card scheme gives you a free days fishing after 7 visits.

Types of Fish:

Number of Lakes: Two

Rules/Bans: There is a no keep nets policy to ensure the fish are kept in good condition. No boilies. Barbless hooks only.

Facilities: A static caravan catering for 4 people is now available to rent.

Telephone: 01507 328777
Mob: 0790 771 2413
www.alvinghamlakes.co.uk

9

Ashby Park
West Ashby, Horncastle.

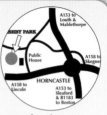

Ticket Price: Day ticket £6.00.
Concessions to campers.

Directions: 1.5 miles north of Horncastle between the A158 & A153.

Description: There are seven lakes here at Ashby Park set in seventy acres of beautiful countryside. Parking is behind most pegs which makes it an excellent venue for the disabled angler. It is stocked on a regular basis and has many species. This David Bellamy Gold Conservation Award Park offers you a friendly and informal atmosphere, peace, tranquillity, good walks a diversity of wildlife. The chance to enjoy a few truly relaxing days away from the crowd and enjoy a peaceful days fishing or a holiday retreat.

Types of Fish: Top weights of carp 25lb 3oz, chub 5lb 8oz, roach and rudd 3lb 1oz, tench 9lb, bream 14lb 6oz, pike 28lb, perch 3lb 4oz.

Facilities:

Rules/Bans: Barbless hooks only. All children must be accompanied by an adult. No carp to be kept in keepnets.

Number of Lakes: Seven

Telephone: 01507 527966   **Sat Nav:** LN9 5PP

Bainside Coarse Fishery
Bainside Nurseries, Roughton Road, Kirkby on Bain.

Ticket Price: Day ticket £5.00. £1.00 for an extra rod. Concessions £4.00. Evening ticket £3.00.

Directions: From Horncastle take the A153 heading towards Coningsby. After about five miles turn right to Kirkby on Bain. Look for signs for the fishery.

Description: This fishery is set at the side of the River Bain and is around two acres in size. The car park is adjacent to the lake with level easy access to most pegs. With its long island strip and water lily beds there are plenty of features to target. The lake contains a good mix of fish species and has something for everyone, with all methods working well.

Types of Fish: Carp, Grass carp, tench, crucian, rudd, roach, bream and chub.

Rules/Bans: Ground bait in moderation. Keepnets are allowed but must be dipped first. Barbless hooks only. No dogs. See further rules on-site.

Number of Lakes: One   **Telephone:** 01526 352050

Facilities: Snack bar, car parking, disabled toilet. Space for 5 Caravans. **Holiday lodge available.** Small matches accepted.

Sat Nav: LN10 6YL

Bain Valley Fisheries

North Road Farm, Tattershall Thorpe, Lincolnshire.

SAT NAV LN4 4PQ

Ticket Price: £6.00. 2 rods £8.00.
Concessionary Day Ticket £5.00. £2.00 extra rod
Night Fishing must be pre-booked. 24 hours £20.00.

Directions: Situated just off the A153 on the B1192
Tattershall/Coningsby to Woodhall Spa road. Once in
Tattershall Thorpe turn right just after the Blue Bell Inn onto
Chapel Lane and follow the road to the second bend, North
Road Farm and Bain Valley Fisheries is on the corner.

Description: A picturesque and tranquil fishery situated in the
Bain Valley in the heart of the beautiful Lincolnshire
countryside. Comprising of 10 lakes and offering excellent
carp, coarse and trout fishing. This is a great venue for the
pleasure angler who wants to catch plenty of large fish.

Types of Fish: Carp, tench, crucian, ide, perch, bream, roach,
rudd, and trout.

Rules/Bans: No nuts. Barbless hooks only. Keepnets only in
matches. Landing mats must be used.

Facilities: Parking at pegs on all lakes, toilets, caravan
park with electric hook-up.   P 🚻 ♿ 🚐 🔑5

Number of Lakes: Ten
www.bainvalleyfisheries.co.uk   **Telephone:** 01526 342275
                               07779 589210 / 07961 788822
                               Bailiff (Pete) 07956 343346

Blyton Ponds Holiday Park

Adult only holiday venue, Sunnyside Farm, Station Road, Blyton.

SAT NAV DN21 3LE

Ticket Price: Day tickets £6.00 (2 rods). Night fishing strictly by prior arrangement £12.50 - Tel: 01427 628240

Directions: Take the A159 through Gainsborough and Moreton to Blyton. Go down a slight hill through the village until you see a war memorial on the right. Turn on to the B1205 to Kirton in Lindsey. Take the next right turn and then the very next right turn and Blyton Ponds is located on your left approx 70 metres.

Description: The fishery consists of four ponds, Pond (A) has 15 pegs, Pond (B) has 12 pegs. These two ponds are connected by a narrow channel. Pond (C and D) which are only open to residents Monday to Friday, but open for general day ticket fishing at the weekend. There is ample car parking spaces with good disabled access. Most pegs are flat, and all are made of paving slabs.

Types of Fish: All four ponds are well stocked with a great variety of fish, including common carp, mirror carp, crucian carp, ghost carp, chub, barbel, golden and green tench, roach, rudd, perch, and bream.

Rules/Bans: No keepnets. No groundbait. No hemp or boilies. Barbless hooks.

Number of Lakes: Four

Facilities: Cafe & tackle shop, toilets. Excellent self catering 2 or 3 bed static caravan, or bed & breakfast chalet available.

Telephone: 01427 628240 for a brochure.

www.blytonponds.co.uk   e-mail: info@blytonponds.co.uk

13

Butterswood Fisheries
Soff Lane, Goxhill.

SAT NAV LN19 7NA

Ticket Price: Day tickets £5.00, Concessions £3.00
Extra rods £1.00 (Open all year, dawn till dusk.)

Directions: Head towards Barton-upon-Humber on the A15.
Turn right at second crossroads onto College Road
(signposted East Halton). After about 2 miles take your
second left. Turn immediately to your right and go through
the green gates, the fishery is on the left.

Description: There are three lakes to try, the largest has 30
pegs and has an average depth of 6 feet. There are a few
double pegs which are very popular. The other two lakes
are smaller and have 16 and 17 pegs with some doubles.
Most pegs are suitable for the disabled.

Types of Fish: Carp to 28lb, tench and chub to 7lb, roach and
rudd to 2lb, perch to 3lb.

Rules/Bans: Barbless hooks only. No floating baits. No nut
baits/hemp/tares. No litter. Unhooking mats and landing nets
must be used at all times. No keep nets, except in the tench
pond. No children under 14 without an adult

Number of Lakes: Three

Facilities: Car park, toilets,
hot & cold drinks. Some baits are sold on site.
Cottage and bungalows available for holidays.

Telephone: 01469 533098   **Sat Nav:** LN19 7NA

Bradley Ponds
Bradley Road, Waltham.

SAT NAV DN37 OAL

Ticket Price: Day Tickets - £5.00. OAP Tickets - £4.00
Under 12's £3.00 (must be accompanied by an adult).
2 Rods £7.00

Directions: From A46 pass Morrisons and stay on the road
until you come to a roundabout. Take the third exit onto
Bradley Road, stay on the road until you pass Bradley
Woods, then follow signs for Bradley Ponds.

Description: Bradley Ponds has two lakes covering 10 acres.
Its great for both the course and carp angler, everyone is
made to feel welcome by Tony and his team who are on site
if you need help or advice.

Types of Fish: Small Pond: Tench 5lb, Rudd 1lb, Roach 2lb,
Perch 3.5lb, Blue Orf 2lb, Golden Orf 4lb, Chub 4lb, Barbel
7lb, Crucians 3lb, Bream 3lb, Carp 16lb
Big Pond: Tench 6lb, Golden Tench 3lb, Rudd 1lb, Roach
2lb, Perch 3.5lb, Blue Orf 2lb, Golden Orf 4lb, Chub 4lb,
Barbel 7lb, Crucians 3lb, Bream 6lb, Carp 31lb.

Rules/Bans: No night fishing. No dog meat or cat meat.
No braided line. No floating baits. No fires.
No dogs on the fishery.
Only feed pellets bought from the site shop to be used.

Facilities: On-site shop selling bait,   **Number of Lakes:** Two
tackle, hot and cold drinks and snacks.

Telephone: 01472 360907

Claxby Fishery

Claxby Grange Farm, Claxby, Market Rasen.

SAT **LN8 3YR** NAV

Ticket Price: Day tickets £5.00. Concessions and school children £4.00. Evening ticket (after 5pm) £4.00.
Season Tickets £75.00 Concession Season Tickets £60.00

Description: The fishery consists of three ponds that are well stocked with a variety of fish. Both common and mirror carp reach 20lbs and are in excellent condition. The ponds close on 30th September and reopen on 1st of February.

Directions:

Types of Fish: Common and mirror carp, crucian carp, tench,bream, roach and rudd.

Rules/Bans: No night fishing. Barbless hooks only.
No fish over 2lbs in keepnets.
All rubbish to be taken home.

Number of Lakes: Three

Facilities: Car park, toilets, disabled access

Sat Nav: Claxby Grange Farm

Telephone:
Coarse fishing Ponds: 01673 828253
Trout Fishing Lake: 07977 494420

16.5lb Comm

16

Duck Ponds

Besthorpe Road, North Scarle, Lincoln.

Ticket Price: Day Fishing £5.00 Concessions £4.00 (Ages 10 - 16, Senior Citizens) Under 10s £3.00. Caravan Rates - £15 per night or £20 to include two fishing.

Directions: From Newton on Trent take the A1133 south. When you reach Besthorpe turn left onto Sand Lane. After a couple of miles this Lane becomes Besthorpe Road. Look out for the fishery on your right.

Description: Two well stocked ponds, Ye Old Pond and Willows Pond. Ye Old Pond which is a quiet secluded 26 peg pond contains a variety of fish with carp that reach 20lb. The Willows is slightly bigger with 31 pegs and has been extensively stocked with barbel and carp. This pond is surrounded by camping pitches for easy access.

Types of Fish: Roach, perch, barbel, carp and tench.

Rules/Bans: No ground bait. No night fishing. Barbless hooks only. No fish to be taken away. No boilies. No fish over 3lb in keep nets.

Number of Lakes: Two   **Sat Nav:** LN6 9EZ

Facilities:

Telephone: 01522 779053 or 07908 646218

9

Fenlake Fishery
Fen Lane, Metheringham.

SAT NAV LN4 3AQ

Ticket Price: Day tickets £5.00. Only one rod or pole is allowed. £3.50 after 4.30pm in the summer.

Directions: When you reach Metheringham, take the B1189 Lincoln Road. Turn opposite the fire station on to Fen Lane. Go over the railway bridge and look for the fishery on your right hand side.

Description: Fenlake is a well stocked 20 peg lake. Most silver fish species can be found in this water. Their is one island which can be reached with a pole. If you can get a peg that lets you reach the corner, this is where the carp seem to be. If you can't reach the island try fishing close to the margin reeds. Red maggot for the roach, meat or sweetcorn for the larger fish. Heard great reports about match weights on this lake. Winning weights over 250lbs!! Meg Lake, a new 19 peg lake with a sunken island has recently opened, giving plenty of room for pleasure fishing. This is a great venue for the pleasure angler who wants to build there confidence handling plenty of large fish.

Types of Fish: Roach, rudd, bream, tench, perch, and carp.

   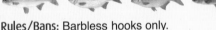

Rules/Bans: Barbless hooks only.
No keepnets except in matches. See further rules on site.

Facilities:

Sat Nav: LN4 3AQ

Number of Lakes: Two   **Telephone:** 07833 753392   10

Froghall Fisheries

Furze Lane, Legbourne, Louth.

SAT NAV **LN11 8LR**

Ticket Price: £6.00 for 1 rod & £10.00 for 2 rods
OAP's & Disabled £5.00 for 1 rod
Children under 16 years old £4.00 per rod
24 Hour Fishing by arrangement £15.00 for up to 2 rods.

Directions: Take the A157 to Legbourne, Frog Hall lies to the north of the village on its eastern edge.

Description: There are three mature fishing lakes, the largest being over one and a half acres. Teeming with the finest specimen fish with an abundance of carp in excess of 25lb. There is plenty of rudd and roach up to 2lb. A good head of bream and tench plus perch up to 5lb. Froghall is an ideal venue for a cracking days fishing or even a weeks sport while staying in one of the individual log cabins or on the camping and touring caravan area. Excellent concrete fishing platforms which are close to the car park making this fishery ideal for the disabled angler.

Rules/Bans: Barbless hooks only. No keep nets except in matchers. See on site for further rules.

Facilities: Car park, toilet block and shower room. Cafe and tackle shop on site. New log cabins to hire. Electric hook up for touring caravans available. Grass area for camping.

Number of Lakes: Three
Telephone: 01507 354984

o.5 Acre Lake
Log Cabins
Caravans
Frog Hall
Tents
1.5 Acre Lake
Restaurant & Shop
0.5 Acre Lake
Parking
Ornamental Pond

Grange Park
Grange Park Leisure Complex, Messingham.

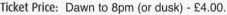

SAT NAV DN17 3PP

Ticket Price: Dawn to 8pm (or dusk) - £4.00.
Under 14s - £3.00. Twilight Rate: 4pm till 8pm £3.00

Directions: Turn off the M180 at the Scunthorpe Junction 3 exit and travel along the M181 for two miles. Take the A18 signposted Ashby. Turn off onto the A159, follow this road to a crossroads. Turn right signposted East Butterwick, don't follow the Messingham sign. Grange Park is just past Messingham Sands fishery, on your left hand side.

Description: This single lake is around two acres in size and is part of the leisure facilities available. One side of the lake is next to the golf course which is not fishable. I spoke to a man from Rotherham who had been fishing from 5am with his son and between them had caught 40 good sized carp. Most methods work here with depths of 3-4 feet in the margins and nearing 20 feet in the middle.

Types of Fish: Carp, roach, bream, and tench.

Rules/Bans: No keepnets. Barbless hooks only. No groundbait. No litter. (Under 14s must be accompanied by an adult).

Facilities: Car parking, toilets, disabled access, cafe, caravan hook ups.

Number of Lakes: One

Telephone: 01724 762945   **Sat Nav:** DN17 3PP

13

Grooby's Pit

Bridgefoot Farm, Steeping Rd, Thorpe St Peter.

SAT NAV PE24 4QU

Ticket Price: £5.00 Adults. £4.00 Concessions (Over 65, Under 16, Students & Disabled). Evening Ticket (4pm till Dusk) £4.00 Adults. £3.00 Concessions.

Directions: Grooby's Pit is situated next to Thorpe Culvert Railway Station.

Description: This is a friendly, family run site with a 2 acre well established fishing lake. Stocked with Bream, Tench, Roach, Barbel, Carp, Chub, Perch, Rudd, Skimmers & Eels. Grooby's Pit is a mature lake, with 30 individual pegs, most with parking at the side. Many anglers come here to catch the large bream that are present and enjoy the peaceful surroundings.

Rules/Bans: There is no bait bans – Except for no cat or dog meat. Groundbait through a cupping kit or feeder only, no balling in. All nets MUST be dipped before entry. See full list of rules on site.

Number of Lakes: One

Facilities: Camping and Caravanning club site.

Telephone: 07427 137463

Hatton Lake
Horncastle Rd, Hatton.

Ticket Price: Day tickets £5.00

Directions: Leave Lincoln on the A158 and head towards Wragby. The fishery is on the left of the main road (A158) between Wragby and Horncastle.

Description: This well kept small fishery has two islands to target plus many other features. It has 26 well spaced pegs with most being suitable for the disabled angler. Try fishing as close to the islands as that's where many of the larger carp are holding up. A small square of meat or sweetcorn works well in the warmer months. If you're struggling for bites switch to a red maggot for the plentiful rudd.

Types of Fish: Carp, tench, roach, rudd, perch and crucian

Rules/Bans: Barbless hooks only. No groundbait. No children under 14yrs unless with an adult.

Number of Lakes: One

Facilities: Car park and toilets.

Telephone: 01673 858682 (8am to 7pm)   Sat Nav: LN8 5QE

Hill View Park
Skegness Road, Hogsthorpe.

Ticket Price: Day tickets £6.00. Tickets purchased from the cafe. Open from March to December, seven days per week from 7:00am to 9:00pm (or dawn till dusk).

Directions: From Skegness, take the A52 heading towards Mablethorpe. The fishery entrance is signposted on the left before Hogsthorpe Village.

Description: This venue at Hogsthorpe has four lakes, one of which is for site residents only. All ages and abilities are welcome here and all should catch. Try the margins for the carp with small pieces of meat or sweetcorn. With depths to around six feet the two acre carp lake has carp to 28lbs. The much smaller lake (around 3/4 of an acre) also has some good carp to 20lbs, along with most other species of silver fish. A great all round leisure park with beautiful fishing lakes.

Types of Fish: Carp, tench, bream, roach, crucian, perch and rudd.

Rules/Bans: No keepnets. Bait bans in force (check for details).
All nets must be dipped and barbless hooks must be used.

Number of Lakes: Four

Facilities: Car parking, toilets, good access for the disabled angler, waterfront cafe and bar. LUXURY MODERN HOLIDAY COTTAGES TO RENT.

Telephone: 01754 872979   **Sat Nav:** PE24 5NR   16

23

Hunters Lodge Fishery
Church Street, Elsham, Brigg.

SAT NAV DN20 0RG

Ticket Price: Silver fish pond: £5.00. Concessions £4.00.
Carp Ponds: From £6.00 a day, £12 a night.

Directions: From the M180 Junction 5 head into the village of
Elsham. Take your first right onto Front Street, quickly
followed by a left turn into Maltkiln Lane. Follow this road for
approx 400yds. Turn left on the right hand bend, onto a
small lane which leads to the lakes.

Description: This four lakes fishery is set in the beautiful surroundings of the Lincolnshire Wolds. Willows, Kestrel and
Kingfisher lakes are specimen carp waters with fish up to
32lbs. Heron Pond is a silver fish pond and contains many
different species. It has tench, rudd, chub, ide, crucian carp,
bream and barbel. Night fishing is available on all ponds.

Number of Lakes: Four

Facilities: The tackle shop is well stocked,
including maggots and worms.
Cafe is available on site.

Rules/Bans: Barbless hooks must be used on all ponds.
Keepnets must not be used in any of the specimen lakes.
No carp sacks. No fires. All rubbish must be placed in the
bins provided. Unhooking mats must be used. No fishing
rods to be left un-attended. A full list of rules can be found
on there website. **www.hunterslodgefishery.com**

Telephone: 01652 680691 / 07701054883

17

24

Kingfisher Lodge
Hibaldstow, Brigg.

Ticket Price: Day tickets £4.00 one rod. £1.00 per extra rod.

Directions: Leave the M180 at junction 4 and take the A15 to Lincoln. After 3 miles turn left to Hibaldstow. Turn right continuing on the B1206. Take your next left (Hibaldstow Bridge). After just under a mile turn left and you will find the fishery 300 metres on your right.

Description: This 3 acre fishing lake has 35 pegs many suitable for the disabled angler. The depth is between 3 and 8 feet. Parking behind each peg makes life very easy on the back, if like me you have too much tackle. This lake is stocked with quality fish of most species.

Types of Fish: Carp to over 24lbs, bream and tench to 6lbs, chub to 6lb, perch to 3lb, roach and rudd to 2lb.

Rules/Bans: No night fishing. No carp in nets. No groundbait except in feeder. Barbless hooks only.

Number of Lakes: One

Facilities: Car parking, caravans welcome, toilets.

Telephone: 01652 652210   Sat Nav: DN20 9PJ

Lake Ross

Dozens Bank, West Pinchbeck, Spalding.

Ticket Price: Day tickets £7.00 per rod. (Dawn to Dusk)
Senior Citizens £5.00.   £4.00 per evening (4pm to Dusk)

Directions: Lake Ross is easily located 2.5 miles west of
Spalding on the A151 to Bourne in the country village of
Pode Hole.

Description: The lake is set within a small family run caravan
park and is well stocked with a variety of course fish.
The pegs are well maintained and have reed bed margins
which are excellent for targeting the good sized carp on a
summers evening. Access is available to all banks with
plenty of pegs and stages suitable for the disabled angler.
A great venue for both the experienced and novice angler.

Types of Fish: Carp, tench, roach, rudd, chub, and barbel.

Rules/Bans: Barbless hooks only. No floating baits.
Groundbait in open end feeder only. No boilies.

Number of Lakes: One

Facilities: Car parking, toilets, camping & caravan hook-ups.
Food and drink available from the sites clubhouse.

Telephone: 01775 761690   **Sat Nav:** PE11 3NA

Lakeside Caravan Park

Barlings Lane, Langworth.

SAT LN3 5DF NAV

Ticket Price: Adult ticket £5.00. Concessions £3.00

Directions: If you approach Langworth on the A158 from Lincoln, turn right and continue into Langworth village. Go past the church on your right. Take the next turning right, this is "Barlings Lane" with brown tourist sign for "LAKESIDE CARAVAN PARK", turn down Barlings Lane, about ½ mile down lane, past the cemetery on your left. You will see another brown tourist sign opposite our entrance.

Description: At Lakeside there are two fishing lakes with very different environments for you to choose from. Match Lake is largely open and deeper than Kingfisher which is shallower and more covered from surrounding bushes. They are stocked with a great variation of Carp (Crucian, Common, Mirror, Ghost etc), Bream, Tench, Roach, Rudd, Perch and many more ranging in sizes from fry upto 20lb+. All fish are very well looked after by fishermen due to the relatively strict rules about nets and general handling of the fish.

Rules/Bans: Barbless hooks only. No Keep nets. Landing nets must be soaked before use. Baits that are allowed, branded Carp pellets, meats, worms, maggots, bread and corn to be used as baits as they do not harm the fish and are generally the best baits for catching the fish in the lakes.
See other rules on site.

Facilities:

Number of Lakes: Two   **Telephone:** 01522 753200

Lakeside Fishery
Lincoln Road, Baumber.

Ticket Price: Day tickets £5.00. Concessions £4.00.

Directions: From Horncastle take the A158 signposted Lincoln. Pass through the village of Baumber and Lakeside is located about one mile on the right.

Description: Main lake is the largest of the two lakes spanning two acres. This lake is stocked with carp to 35lb. and a good head of tench and bream to 10lb. Ivors Pond has plenty of small fish making it ideal for those just wanting to bag some fish or beginners to the sport. There are roach and rudd to about 1lb.8oz. with tench, bream and koi carp to about 5lbs. Small tench are plentiful and give good sport on light tackle.

Rules/Bans: Nets must be dipped. Barbless hooks only. Unhooking mats to be used. No Carp in keepnets or sacs Fishing only in designated swims. No litter. No radios. No bolt rigs, or fixed leads. Landing nets must be used for all fish. Maximum of 2 rods. No rods to be left unattended at any time. Under 15's must be accompanied by an adult.

Facilities:

Accommodation is available in a Lakeside Cabin, a 30ft static caravan, and their 2 acre camp site.

Telephone: 01507 578330   **Number of Lakes:** Two

Lakeside Leisure

Trunch Lane, Chapel St Leonards.

SAT NAV PE24 5TU

Ticket Price: Day tickets £5.50. 2 rods £9.00

Directions: From Skegness take the A52 north. Go through Ingoldmells and take your second right on to Trunch Lane. Continue to the sea wall and follow the tourist information signs to the lakes.

Description: There are four lakes to chose from, starting with the Boating Lake which is 3.5 acres and holds the larger carp up to 36lbs and reported catfish to 69lb. Kingfisher Lake has been stocked with trout which have to be returned. It also has carp to 8lb and a good head of silver fish. Horseshoe Lake has an island and reed beds to target carp again to 24lbs plus some lovely tench. The last and smallest pond is the Golf Pond which is heavily stocked with most species including small barbel. If thats not enough you can try sea fishing which is only 50 yards away.

Types of Fish: 27 species including bream, barbel, carp, chub, golden orfe, rudd, tench, perch, roach and trout.

Facilities:

Well stocked tackle shop on-site. Childrens amusements.

Rules/Bans: No fish over 4lbs in keepnets.
No cat or dog meat. Barbless hooks only.

Number of Lakes: Four   **Telephone:** 01754 872631

Email: lakesideadam@yahoo.co.uk

22

Langdale Lakes
Station Road, Langworth, Nr Lincoln.

SAT
LN3 5BB
NAV

Ticket Price: Both Willow Lake and Lily Lake are £5 Mon-Fri. (£7 Weekends) 1 or 2 rods. £1 per extra rod.
Willow Lake 24hrs £15.00.   Lily Lake 24hrs £20.00

Directions: Take the A158 from Lincoln heading east. You will reach Langworth after a couple of miles. The fishery is on your left-hand side. Keep a look out for the fishery sign.

Description: Willow Lake is 1.4 acres in size, with tree lined margins. This mixed Carp and Coarse fishing lake is very well stocked with Mirrors & Commons, the largest fish now being around 27lb, so this lake is also suitable for the serious carp angler. Together with tench to 7lb, bream to 9lb. and a good head of crucian carp plus roach, perch and chub that are sure to provide hours of quality fishing. The 1.6 acre Lily Lake has been established for over 100 years and has been fully re-stocked with a mix of beautiful Mirror Carp and Common Carp to 20lbs.

Rules/Bans: Barbless hooks only. No keepnets. No tiger nuts Under 16's must be accompanied by a responsible adult. Goundbait may only be used on a feeder or method rig. No loose groundbaiting is allowed. See other rules on site.

Number of Lakes: Two

Facilities: Parking, toilets, caravan pitches, camping

Telephone:
Tony or Karen on: 01522 752414

High Quality Bed & Breakfast rooms available.

23

Mary Wood Fisheries
Stamford Road, Little Bytham.

Ticket Price: Day ticket £6.00 (Adult). £4.00 (Junior/OAP)

Directions:

Description: Mary Wood Lake is over 150 years old. It covers some 2 acres and most of the 54 pegs have a feature to fish against. Stocked with roach, rudd, perch, tench, crucians, chub, gudgeon, skimmers, eels, carp and trout.

Meadow View Lake was constructed in 2003. It is about 1½ acres in area and has been designed with the pole angler in mind. It has 58 pegs and an island the full length of the lake The fish in this lake are mainly carp from a few ounces to 10lb in weight. There are also a few roach, rudd and trout.

Rules/Bans: No keepnets, barbless hooks only.

Number of Lakes: Two

Facilities: There is a cottage in Aunby available for rental.

Telephone: 07966 472015

Messingham Sands

Butterwick Road, Messingham, Nr Scunthorpe.

SAT NAV **DN17 3PN**

Ticket Price: Day tickets £6.00. Concessions £5.00.

Directions: Turn off the M180 at the Scunthorpe junction 3 exit and travel along the M181 for two miles. Take the A18 signposted Ashby. Turn off onto the A159, follow this road to a crossroads. Turn right signposted East Butterwick, don't follow the Messingham sign. You will find the fishery on your left hand side.

Description: With nine lakes this fishery is one of the biggest in the area. It has 6 match lakes and 3 day ticket lakes. The smaller match lakes have around 20 pegs which makes them ideal for club matches. These are not fishable on a day ticket basis. All lakes are packed with fish and most people were catching on the day I visited. The great plus point is to be able to park behind most pegs.

Types of Fish: Carp, rudd, roach, bream, chub, perch, tench, crucian carp.

Number of Lakes: Six match only, three day ticket lakes.

Rules/Bans: No bait bans but pellets have to be bought on site. No night fishing. Barbless hooks only. No keepnets except in matches.

Facilities: Good parking, shop, cafe, toilets,

Telephone: 01724 763647   **Sat Nav:** DN17 3PN

The North (Day Ticket Lake)

The Oak Tree (Day Ticket Lake)

Tripp (Match Lake)

Mill Farm Leisure
Wrangle Bank, Wrangle, Boston.

SAT NAV PE22 9DT

Ticket Price: Day tickets: 1 Rod £5.00. 2 Rods £7.50.

Directions: From Sibsey take the B1184. After one mile turn right on to Station Road. Follow this road as it turns into Wrangle Bank. Look out for Mill Farm on your right.

Description: Although the lake was only excavated in 2003 the waters appear much older, having matured nicely to provide a host of reed clad bays and plenty of vegetation. The lake occupies approximately 1 acre and the depth varies from 1.5ft down to 9ft. There is a fine stock of hard fighting Carp, some weighing in at over 16lbs. There is specimen tench, perch, rudd and roach all of which are in prime condition. One of the greatest features of fishing at Mill Farm is the peace and tranquillity.

Rules/Bans: Strictly barbless hooks only. All anglers must hold a current and valid rod license. Landing nets must be disinfected on site before use. Due to the size of some of our fish you MUST have and use a landing net at all times. No swinging the fish in. No Keep nets, all fish must be returned to the lake immediately. No ground bait, dog/cat meat, hemp, nuts or bollies. Children under the age of 16 must be supervised at all times whilst fishing.

Number of Lakes: One

Facilities:

Cottage and lodge for hire.

Telephone: 01754 820053

Mill Road Lakes

Mill Road, Addlethorpe, Skegness.

SAT NAV PE24 4TE

Ticket Price: Day Ticket £5.50. Extra Rod £2.00
Evening Ticket (After 4pm) £4.50
OAP/Child upto 14/Disabled £4.50
Night fishing (9pm to 9am) £25.00 (by appointment only)

Directions: From Horncastle head east on the A158. About 5 miles before Skegness you will reach Burgh le Marsh. Turn left to Addlethorpe. You will come across the fishery on you left hand side.

Description: This very attractive fishery consists of two ponds, both contain carp to 25lbs. and tench to around 6lbs. The pegs are nicely spaced with most of them having a reed bed to the side where most people were targeting. They are not big ponds but do seem to suit the pole angler.

Types of Fish: Tench to 6lb. Roach to 1.5lb. Rudd to 1.5lb. Chubb to 2.5lb. Golden Orfe to 3lb. Perch to 2lb. Ghost Carp to 7lb. Mirror Carp to 25lb. Common Carp to 20lb. Crucian Carp to 2.5lb.

Rules/Bans: Barbless hooks only. No ground bait. No boilies or nuts. No trout pellets. Catfood only on hooks. No floating bait. No keepnets. Left over bait not to be thrown in to water.

Number of Lakes: Two   **Telephone:** 07974 852 637

Facilities: Car park, toilets, cafe.   **Sat Nav:** PE24 4TE
Camping and caravaners welcome.

🅿️ 🚻 ♿ 🍔 ☕ 🚐 ⛺   27

Moon Lake Fisheries
Bank Farm, Marsh Lane, Tattershall.

SAT NAV LN4 4JR

Ticket Price: Day tickets £7.00. £1.00 for extra rod. Concessions £6.00. Match booking £7.00 per peg.

Directions: From Sleaford head north on the A153. Go through Billinghay. When you reach the centre of Tattershall turn left onto the B1192. The fishery is about 1 mile on your left hand side. Look out for the small 'brown fish' tourist information signs.

Description: Moon Lake is the largest of the six waters. It is two acres in size with 25 good pegs to fish from. It is circular in shape with a small island in the middle ideal to target the many species available. It offers a great days sport in beautiful surroundings. The other lakes are canal type and are excellent for pole fishing.

Types of Fish: Carp to 25lbs, bream, tench, rudd, barbel, ide and chub.

Rules/Bans: Barbless hooks only. No braid. Ground bait by feeder or pole cup only. No keepnets except in matches.

Number of Lakes: Six

Facilities: Parking, toilets, disabled access.

28

Telephone: 01526 345377   **Sat Nav:** LN4 4JR

Oak Tree Fishery
Station Road (A161), Graizelound, near Haxey.

Ticket Price: Day tickets £5.00. Concessions £4.00.

Directions: The fishery is located just off the A161 at Graizelound, near Haxey.

[Map showing: To Haxey, To Doncaster, To Owston Ferry, A161, Oak Tree Fishery, Warping Drain, To Misterton & Gainsborough]

Description: The lake carries a fine head of general coarse stock and our young carp are growing fast. There are plenty in the 7-8lb bracket. It has 26 pegs, all of which are easily accessible from the perimeter track. Pegs 23 and 24 have been specially designed to accommodate disabled anglers and are ideal for wheelchair use.

Types of Fish: Oak Tree has been stocked with a fine head of general coarse fish including carp, bream, tench, chub, roach and rudd.

Rules/Bans: Children under 14 years must be accompanied by an adult. Dogs are allowed on site but must be kept on a lead. No keepnets allowed for pleasure fishing. All nets to be dipped on site. Barbless hooks only, no larger than size 12.

Facilities: Some baits are sold on site. **Number of Lakes:** One

Telephone: 01427 891678   29

36

Oakhill Leisure
Swinderby Road, Norton Disney, Lincoln.

Ticket Price: Day tickets £7.00 (2 rods). £8.00 (3 rods) 24hrs £15.00.

Directions: Conveniently situated off the A46 between Lincoln and Newark on Trent. Look for the signpost to Thurlby & Norton Disney.

Description: This mature 5 acre lake is able to accommodate 40 pegs approximately. Well shielded by bushes and trees the lake is fully stocked with carp, tench, rudd and bream. Most anglers come for the carp, as there are quite a few around the 20lb mark and one or two that reach 35lb. Set in beautiful countryside perfectly located for those who enjoy walking and cycling as well as fishing.

Types of Fish: Carp to 35lbs, tench, rudd and bream.

Rules/Bans: Maximum of 3 rods per angler. No keepnets. No tiger nuts or peanuts. Barbless hooks only.

Number of Lakes: One

Facilities: Parking, toilets, camping, caravans welcome.

Telephone: 01522 868771   Sat Nav: LN6 9QG

Oasis Lakes
Warren Rd, North Somercotes, Louth.

Ticket Price: 16+yrs £6.00 per day for one rod. 11-15 yrs £5 per day for one rod and under 11yrs £4 per day for one rod. Concessions £4 per day for one rod. Additional rods are charged at an additional 50% of the appropriate day rate for your age. The Carp Lake is £6 per day for one rod regardless of age and a further £4 for a 2nd rod.

Directions: Take the B1200 from Louth. At the A1031, turn left and follow the road to the village of North Somercotes. In the village, take the first right after the large caravan park, signposted Oasis Lakes.

Description: Three lakes to chose from, the largest, Carp Lake is 1.8 acres with an average depth of 9 feet. Double figure carp upto 38lbs and a massive one day record pleasure catch of 525lb. Slightly smaller is Roadside Lake which has mainly silver fish. Island Lake is just under an acre and is also the shallowest at 5 feet. This lake has most species and is more suitable for the younger angler.

Rules/Bans: Barbless hooks only. No trout pellets. No fish over 3lbs in keepnets. No spinning.

Facilities: Car parking behind most pegs. Tackle shop. Male and female toilets, cafe. Caravans welcome.

Number of Lakes: Three **Telephone:** 01507 358488

Sat Nav: LN11 7QX

Oham Lakes

Main Road, Maltby le Marsh, Alford.

Ticket Price: Day Ticket £6.00 (2 rods £10.00). Concessions £3.00. Children under 10 – Free of charge when accompanied by a paying adult.

Directions: From Louth follow the signs for Mablethorpe on the A157. This will take you through several villages before you come into Maltby le Marsh. At the T-junction in Maltby turn left and the fishery entrance is a short way down the road on your left.

Description: The fishing is on three pools, one developed for the younger angler where it's a fish ever few minutes and the other two holding everything from silver fish through barbel and chub to mirror and common carp to over 30lbs. This fishery has developed a lot over recent years and now has an excellent cafe and well stocked tackle shop.

Types of Fish: Common, mirror, grass and leather carp. Bream, roach, rudd, tench, chub, barbel and crucian.

Rules/Bans: Barbless hooks only. No keepnets.

Number of Lakes: Three

Facilities: Ample parking, toilets, tackle shop, cafe, camping, caravan hook-up. Holiday static caravans and cabins for hire.

Telephone: 01507 450623   **Sat Nav:** LN13 0JP

Peacock Waters
Fen Road, Timberland.

Ticket Price: £5.00 for 1 rod, £2.00 per extra rod (max of 2 rods when busy). £3.00 - under 12 years old.

Directions: Take the B1191 from Woodhall Spa. After around 5 miles you will reach a village called Martin. Turn left, sign posted Timberland. In the centre of Timberland turn left into Fen Road. The fishery is well signed on your left hand side.

Description: This two acre former brick pit is very deep in parts. Float fishing sweetcorn works well for the tench and hair-rigged meat will tempt the carp which can weigh up to 29lbs. The best swims are near the island or any of the overhanging willow trees. Plenty of bream and skimmers can be caught on maggot if you can get through the greedy large perch.

Types of Fish: Tench to 6lb, carp to 29lb, bream, large perch, chub, roach, rudd, eels and crucian.

Rules/Bans: Barbless hooks only. No carp in keepnets. See other rules on site.

Number of Lakes: One

Facilities: Static Caravans and Holiday Barn available, as well as touring caravan pitches.

Telephone: 01526 378059

www.peacockwaters.co.uk

Rainwater Lake
Low Road, Croft Bank, Skegness.

SAT NAV PE24 4RQ

Ticket Price: Day tickets £4.00. Concessions £3.50.

Directions: From Boston head towards Skegness on the A52. Two miles after you pass the Wainfleet Bypass turn left at Lomax's Garage. The lake is 100 metres on the left.

Description: The prominent species in this well stocked lake are carp, rudd and tench with the biggest catch being a massive 29lb. mirror carp. There are plenty of other silver fish present making this lake ideal for both the novice and experienced angler. The pegs are well spaced out giving a feeling of seclusion.

Types of Fish: Rudd, roach, bream, tench, perch, and carp.

Rules/Bans: Barbless hooks only. No keepnets.
No groundbait. No bloodworm or hemp.
Children under 14 must be accompanied by an adult.

Number of Lakes: One

Facilities: Car parking, toilets, Caravan facilities available. Rainwater Lake offers a selection of accommodation to suit all tastes, Caravans, Premier Flats and Cottage.

Telephone: 01754 765783   **Sat Nav:** PE24 4RQ

Roach Farm Park
Burgh Road, Skegness.

Ticket Price: Day ticket £6.00. Children under 14 yrs and OAPs £4.00. After 4.30pm £4.00 and £2.50

Directions: Situated on the main road it is easily found on the A158 between Skegness and Burgh Le Marsh. It is signposted from Burgh Le Marsh and you would have to pass Roach Farm Park in order to reach Skegness.

Description: There are plenty of pegs that are well spaced and a decent size, so more than one angler can fish off each. This is an added bonus for younger fishermen as it means they can sit next to dad in safety and learn how to catch those 20 pounders that he is always talking about.

Types of Fish: Currently stocked with roach, rudd, tench, bream, perch and chub also numerous species of carp including mirror, ghost, hybrid, common and leather.

Rules/Bans: Barbless hooks. Nets must be dipped. No carp or tench in keepnets. No ground bait, boilies or nut

Number of Lakes: Three

Facilities: Parking, tackle shop, toilets, caravan hook-up. Holiday accommodation in static caravans available.

Telephone: 01754 898049   Sat Nav: PE25 2LA

Rosewood Fishery

Blankney Fen, Woodhall Spa.

SAT NAV LN10 6XH

Ticket Price: Day tickets £5.00. One rod only. No concessions.

Directions: 14 miles south east of Lincoln City, 4 miles north west of Woodhall Spa and 3 miles off the B1191 Woodhall Spa to Martin Road.

Description: Whether you use a rod or pole, are experienced or a novice this lake suits most anglers. There is good access to most of the 20 pegs, with parking adjacent. The lake is oval in shape with an island situated at one end. Try and get a peg near the island. If you wish to escape from everything and enjoy a good days fishing in a lovely peaceful location then try this fishery.

Types of Fish: Their are common, ghost, mirror and a few ornamental carp. Plenty of bream, roach, rudd and perch and even large fan-tailed goldfish.

Rules/Bans: Barbless hooks only. No keepnets or ground bait. No bite alarms. No night fishing. Children under 16 years of age must be accompanied by an adult.

Facilities: Three static caravans are for hire.

Number of Lakes: One

Telephone: 01526 378628
Mobile: 07808 167369

43

Royston Waters

Eagle Road, North Scarle, Lincoln.

SAT
LN6 9EN
NAV

Ticket Price: Day tickets £6.00

Directions: Head out of Lincoln on the ring road (A46).
At the Whisby junction turn right. Follow the road through
Eagle Moor until you reach a village called Eagle.
Turn right and follow the road for about a mile. Turn left and
go past the entrance to Lowfields Caravan Park. Royston
Waters is the next entrance on your left.

Description: Royston has a variety of depths and banks with
water from 4ft to 9ft deep. Many features including hanging
willow trees, reed banks and two islands. A clay bottomed
lake with lots of colour. There are plenty of carp between
fingerlings and 18lb, tench upto 4 1/2 lb, small bream and
plenty of silverfish.

Types of Fish: Common carp, mirror carp, leather carp, ghost
carp, golden orf, green tench, silver bream, roach, rudd and
gudgeon.

Rules/Bans:

DAY RULES

No keep nets	No ground bait
No barbed hooks	No braided line
No hook larger than 14	No boilies
Handle all fish with care	No litter
No trout pellets / carp pellets permitted	

🚻   P   37⚡

Number of Lakes: One   **Facilities:** Parking, toilets.

Telephone: 07554 695427   Match bookings are available

Rush Field Lakes

Station Road (B1178), Potterhanworth, Lincoln.

SAT NAV LN4 2DX

Ticket Price: Day tickets cost £5 per person.
Season Tickets are available for £50 per year starting from the 1st of April to 31st March the following year.

Directions: The fishery is situated just outside the village of Potterhanworth, which is about 7 miles south of Lincoln. Just off the B1178 which runs into Potterhanworth.

Description: There are two lakes which are open for day tickets. The larger of the two lakes has 33 pegs and is horse shoe shaped. It is stocked with a large variety of coarse fish including roach, bream, perch and carp.
The smaller lake has 10 pegs and is predominantly stocked with carp although there are a few small roach and skimmer bream. Opening times are from dawn till dusk throughout the year and keep nets are not permitted after 6pm.

Rules/Bans: Keep nets are strictly not to be used after 6pm. Barbless Hooks only. Ground bait to be put in by pole cup or feeder, not thrown in.

Number of Lakes: Two   **Sat Nav:** LN4 2DX

Facilities: 38

Telephone: Contact Tim or Stuart on 01522 793169

45

Saltfleetby fisheries

Main Rd, Saltfleetby, Louth.

Ticket Price: Day ticket £7.00 one rod. £9.00 two rods Concessions £5.00.

Directions: The fishery is situated 6 miles east of Louth on the B1200. Between Louth and Mablethorpe.

Description: This Fishery has three well stocked lakes set in natural and sheltered surroundings. The Main Lake is an old brick pit which is two acres and has a depth of between 4ft and 20ft. Island Pond is one and a half acres, Silver Pond is just under an acre. Both these ponds are around 4ft deep with some great margins to fish close to.

Types of Fish: Bream 7lb, tench 7lb, carp to 25lb, rudd 3lb, crucian carp 2lb, roach 1 1/2lb, perch to 3lb and chub.

Rules/Bans: Barbless hooks only. All nets to be dipped. Groundbait in feeder or pole cup only. No large carp in keepnets.

Number of Lakes: Three

Facilities: Car parking, toilets, bait and tackle shop, food and drinks available, touring caravan site. Static caravans are available for hire.

Telephone: 01507 338272   **Sat Nav:** LN11 7SS

Swan Lake

Culvert Rd, Wainfleet, Skegness.

SAT NAV PE24 4NJ

Ticket Price: Day tickets £6.00 per rod. 2 rod limit 7am till dusk.

Directions: Signposted on the A52, between Boston and Skegness.

Description: There are two lakes to chose from. The largest lake, Swan Lake is 2 acres and has been established over 100 years. The second lake, Leaver Lake is about 1 acre with depths that vary, its deepest being 8 feet in the middle. Both are stocked with a variety of quality fish. Pleasure weights of 50lbs. are not uncommon. Fish pole close to margins or reed beds for Tench, Carp and Barbell. Rudd and Roach taken close to surface on maggot and caster. Method feeder with corn, meat or pellet never fails when the going gets tough!

Types of Fish: Carp, tench, roach, rudd, barbel, perch and crucian

Rules/Bans: Barbless hooks only. No carp or barbel in nets. Handle fish with respect.

Number of Lakes: Two

Facilities: Four berth luxury caravans all with there own lock-up tackle sheds are for hire.

Telephone: 01754 881456   **Sat Nav:** PE24 4NJ

40

Sycamore Lakes

Skegness Road, Burgh le Marsh, Skegness.

SAT NAV **PE24 5LN**

Ticket Price: Day ticket £6.00 one rod. £10.00 two rods. OAP's, Disabled £5.00. Under 16yrs £4.00 one rod.

Directions: From Skegness head west on the A158. Sycamore Lakes are on your left just before you reach Burgh le Marsh.

Description: There are four heavily stocked fishing lakes. Three of them have carp over 25lb, tench, rudd, roach and perch being the prominent species. Island Lake is a two acre water with a depth of 5-6 feet with a deeper hole at the north end. Specimen Lake is for carp and is popular for ledgering with the majority being 12lb. to 28lb. Roadside Lake is one and a half acres and is 6ft in depth. This lake also has many large fish. Lastly Woodland Lake. This is known as the match lake and is slightly deeper with a small central island and camping areas around it.

Types of Fish: Carp, tench, roach, perch, rudd.

Rules/Bans: No keepnets except in matches. Barbless hooks only. See other rules on site.

Number of Lakes: Four   **Telephone:** 01754 811411

Facilities: Cafe, tackle shop, camping, caravans welcome, disabled toilets. Accommodation in cabins and cottages. The Lakes Bar and Restaurant serves excellent food.

Tetford Country Cottages
East Road, Tetford, Horncastle.

SAT NAV LN9 6QQ

Ticket Price: Fishing is free to cottage guests. Camping & Caravan Club residents on the adjacent camp site can fish the lake at a day rate of £6.00. £3.00 for under 16's.

Directions: From Horncastle head east on the A158. Enter Tetford from Salmonby, turn right after the Cross Keys pub into South Road then first left into East Road. Pass the old sawmill on your left and continue around the bend. The entrance is 150 yards on the left just past Manor Farm house.

Description: The lake is 2.5 acres and an ideal water for the pleasure angler. It is well stocked with bream, tench, roach, rudd, perch, crucian carp, chub and carp to 27lb. There are 43 pegs to chose from. Wheelchair access to four pegs is along a path and then a short distance over grass.

Types of Fish: Perch, carp, rudd, tench, bream, roach, chub and crucian carp

Rules/Bans: Barbless hooks only. Night fishing is only available to cottage residents. No keep nets after dusk. Rod limit of two. No fixed lead or fixed method feeder rigs.Use unhooking mat for carp. Use all bait in moderation. No fish over 2lb to be kept in a keepnet. Dogs allowed but must be kept on lead.

Set in the heart of the Lincolnshire Wolds with fully licensed on site diner, two village pubs and a village shop. All male parties welcome. 12 cottages to rent all over looking the lake.

Facilities: Tackle shop on site.

42 Number of Lakes: Two Telephone: 01507 533276

Thorn House Lakes
Horncastle Road, Boston.

SAT NAV PE22 7DJ

Ticket Price: Day tickets £4.00 on the bank.

Directions: The lakes are two miles outside Boston, heading north on the B1183.

Description: Their are two lakes to try at Thorne House. Both are old brick pits of around a hundred years old. The larger of the two has only six pegs on one bank and is fished by the more skilled angler. The other has 12 pegs and is well stocked with a mixture of silver fish and good quality tench. If you are looking for a carp water this fishery is not for you, but if your looking for a relaxing days fishing give it a try. A friendly, well run small fishery where campers and caravaners are welcome, but it is advisable to book your caravan in before hand.

Types of Fish: Well stocked with tench, bream, crucian carp, perch, roach and rudd.

Rules/Bans: Rules displayed on site. Children are welcome to fish but must be accompanied by an adult.

Facilities: Toilets. Car parking area. To stay overnight you must be a Camping and Caravan Club member, adult only.

     Sat Nav: PE22 7DJ

Telephone: 01205 354301   **Number of Lakes:** Two

Treedale Fishing Mere
& Touring Park, Fen Road, Keal Cotes, Spilsby.

SAT NAV **PE23 4AF**

Ticket Price: Day ticket £6.00. OAP and children accompanied by an adult £5.00. Night fishing (10pm - 10am) £12.00 Pre-booked appointment only.

Directions: From Spilsby take the A16 towards East Keal. Continue along the A16 through West Keal until you reach Keal Cotes. Turn left at The Coach House Pub on to Fen Road. The fishery is on your right.

Description: This water is ideal for most anglers, whether your pole fishing for the roach and rudd or going all out for the large carp that reach a massive 35lbs. The myth of the Keal Eel, which is very big and has teeth! has yet to be caught. I personally would rather catch a few tench at around 7lbs.

Types of Fish: Common and mirror carp to 35lbs, tench to 7lbs, roach, rudd, chubb and a few eels.

Rules/Bans: Barbless hooks, max size 10. No keep nets except in matches. No ground bait. See other rules on site.

Facilities: Toilets, ladies separate. Touring caravan hook-up available. Shower, Tackle shop and Wi-Fi.

 **Number of Lakes:** One

Telephone: 07770 642475 Fax & land line 01790 763131

Trentside Fisheries
Stather Road, Burton upon Stather, Nr Scunthorpe.

Ticket Price: Day Tickets £5.00. Concessions £3.50.
Night fishing is now allowed £15.00 (see bailiff).

Directions: From the Humber Bridge take the A1077 towards
South Ferriby. Stay on this road until you reach a right turn
signposted Thealby/Burton upon Stather (B1430).
At the Sheffield Arms pub go right down Stather Road.
Take first left off Stather Road, then next right towards the
riverbank where you will find the fishery.

Description: A very large catfish is present in this lake which
has been caught three times but has never been landed.
The seven acre lake is set in a beautiful location on the
banks of the River Trent. It has 37 platform pegs suitable for
the disabled angler. Match booking are taken.

Types of Fish: Tench, bream, rudd, roach, pike, eel, catfish
and carp to 34lbs.

Rules/Bans: Barbless hooks only. Keep nets are allowed.
All nets must be dipped before fishing.
No fixed feeders or leads, no loops or paternoster rigs.
JUST FREE RUNNING RIGS. No fires, no dogs, unless
prior consent is given. Ground bait 2 kilos, no fishmeal.
No dog meat or cat meat. No tiger nuts.

Number of Lakes: One   **Facilities:** Parking and toilets

Telephone: 0787 2322704

Sat Nav: Stather Rd, DN15

Water Meadows
Trunch Lane, Chapel St Leonards.

SAT NAV PE24 5UA

Ticket Price: Adults £5.00 for 1 rod - £7.50 2 rods.
Concessions £4.00 1 rod - £6.00 2 rods.
Specimen lake £5.00 per rod, £17.50 per 24hrs.

Directions: Take the A52 north out of Skegness, towards Mabelthorpe. Pass through Ingoldmells and continue towards Chapel St Leonards. Once over the traffic lights for Skegness stadium continue north for about a mile.
Take the first right for Chapel St Leonards and the fishery is about 70 yards on the right hand side.

Description: With four lakes, there's something for everyone. Whether you're into big carp, catfish, pike, match sized carp, bream, tench or big roach. The Moat is a 60 peg match / pleasure lake that contains a variety of different species including Carp to 11lb, Barbel to 4lb, Bream to 7lb, Tench to 6lb as well as lots of big quality Roach, Rudd and Perch. Water Meadows Fishery also caters for the angler looking for the bigger specimen fish. The Rush Pool contains carp to 28lb, Pike to 24lb, and recently stocked Catfish to 20lb.

Rules/Bans: Rules for moat, rush and stock pond, barbless hooks only. See on site for Specimen Lake rules.

Facilities: Well stocked tackle shop on site.
Touring caravan site opposite fishery.

46

Number of Lakes: Four
Telephone: 0771 2223625

Wold View Fisheries
Pelham Road, Claxby.

SAT LN8 3YR NAV

Ticket Price: Day Ticket: £7.00. Pensioners Day Ticket: £5.00
Ladies Day Ticket: £5.00. Juniors Day Ticket: £5.00.

Directions: Head north from Market Rasen on the A46. Turn
right at Claxby (Wold View Tourist Sign). After quarter of a
mile turn right on to Pelham Road. Continue down the road
until you see the fishery sign on your right. (Before the
railway crossing)

Description: With six very different lakes to chose from their is
something for all anglers at Wold View. If like me you want a
more intimate lake then Bronze Pool is the lake for you.
The lake has 19 spacious pegs all with reed bed margins to
fish up to. Stocked with carp, tench, bream and much more,
you will be spoilt for choice by this interesting lake. If you
prefer a larger lake, then try Gold Lake which has 41 pegs
and can be fished from an island via a foot bridge.

Rules/Bans: See the rules on site.

Facilities: On site tackle shop and cafe. Electric hook up for
touring caravans and motorhomes. Disabled pegs, toilets.

P ♿ 🚻 🍴 ☕ 🚐

47

Number of Lakes: Six

Telephone: 07742 220204

Wood Farm

Woodfarm Caravan & Camping, East Fenside, Stickney.

SAT **PE22 8BZ** NAV

Ticket Price: Fishing is free if staying on site. No day tickets.

Directions: Wood Farm can be found north from Stickney Village on the A16 road towards Stickford. You will find the site sign posted.

Description: The lake is well stocked with carp, tench, roach perch and bream. Most anglers were staying in caravans that were only a few feet away from the water, making this site the perfect get away location. There are plenty of reed beds to target the good sized carp which patrol the margins. This is a lovely family run venue with excellent fishing and various other activities.

Types of Fish: Carp, tench, bream, roach and perch.

Rules/Bans: Barbless hooks only. No keepnets.

Facilities: Ladies and gents toilets. Shower block. Two static caravans available for hire. Electic hook up. This site is one of very few that have fire pits giving the place a magical and intimate feel.

Number of Lakes: One

48

Telephone:
Mark or Leigh 01205 480687

55

Woodland Waters

Willoughby Rd, Ancaster, Grantham.

SAT NAV NG32 3RT

Ticket Price: Day ticket 5.00. Concessions £3.50.
Carp fishing £8.00 per day. 24hr ticket £20.00
Additional rods £2.00

Directions: From the south take the B6403. Just past
Colsterworth turn left at Ancaster crossroads. The waters are
300yds. on the right. From the north take the A17 to Newark
and join the B6403. At Ancaster crossroads turn right and
you will find the waters on your right after 300yds.

Description: The biggest of the five lakes at Woodland is
the Specimen Lake at over 14 acres, with an average
depth of 17ft. This lake has mainly carp, bream and pike.
The next largest is the match lake which is 7 acres
and averages 12 feet deep. There are also three smaller
lakes each with about 20 pegs. These are heavily stocked
with carp, roach, tench and rudd. This is a well run site with
excellent fishing, perfect for a few days away.

Types of Fish: Carp to 32lbs., tench to 11lbs., roach to 2lbs.,
perch to 4lbs., pike to 31lbs., bream to 10lbs.
Plenty of crucian and rudd.

Rules/Bans: Barbless hooks only. No keepnets or groundbait
on small lakes. Full rules list is on the back of your day ticket.

Number of Lakes: Five   **Telephone:** 01400 230888

Facilities: Full camping and caravan facilities. Disabled
toilets. Bar and restaurant. Holiday lodges available.

        49

Woodlands Fishery

Ashby Rd, Spilsby.

SAT NAV PE23 5DW

Ticket Price: Day tickets £6.00. Second rod £2.00. Senior citizens and children £5.00. After 4pm £4.00.

Directions: Leave the A16 at the Spilsby junction. After half a mile turn left at the George Hotel into Ashby Road. Follow the road for 1 mile and turn left at the fishery entrance.

Description: My favourite lake is the small 17 peg Ash Lake. Try using meat in the margins for the carp. Woodlands is a 5 lake complex with over 100 pegs, a few custom made for wheelchair anglers. Hawthorn Lake is the newest and largest at around 2 acres and has been heavily stocked with mirror and common carp, plus a mixture of silver fish.

Types of Fish: Carp to 20lbs, crucian carp, tench, bream, rudd, roach and perch.

Rules/Bans: Barbless hooks only. No carp in keepnets or fish over 3lbs. No bloodworm, joker, dog or cat meat. No nuts or boilies. No trout pellets. All nets must be dipped on entry.

Number of Lakes: Five

Facilities: Ample car parking, flush toilets, tackle shop and hot & cold drinks

Telephone: 01790 754252 or 07710 631555

50

Ash Lake

Hawthorn Lake

57

Woodthorpe Hall

Woodthorpe Hall Leisure Park, Nr Alford.

SAT NAV **LN13 0DD**

Ticket Price: Day tickets £6.00. Junior £4.00.
Weekly per person £35.00. Family daily permit £10.00.

Directions: Woodthorpe Hall is situated just off the B1373 about 1.5 miles from Withern village and just over 3 miles from the market town of Alford.

Description: This very picturesque one acre lake is well stocked with tench, roach, rudd, orfe, carp and perch.
The pegs are well spaced out and most have a reed bed to one side, so you can target the good sized tench which like the shade. You can get refreshments close by at the Country Inn which is set within the leisure park

Types of Fish: Tench, roach, rudd, orfe, carp and perch.

Rules/Bans: No loose ground bait to be used except in a reasonable sized bait feeder or small cupping system. Boilies on the hook only. No hemp, or trout pellets to be used. Barbless hooks only. No carp over 3lb. to be kept in keepnets. No night fishing allowed. Maximum of 2 rods per person. No litter to be left. No children under the age of 12 allowed to fish un-supervised.

Facilities: Static caravans and cottages available for holidays.

Telephone: 01507 450294

Number of Lakes: One

River Ancholme
Brandy Wharf

Ticket Price: Day ticket £3.50 on the bank.

Directions: From Lincoln head north on the A15. About 5 miles after the Caenby junction, turn right onto the B1205 signposted Waddingham. Continue through Waddingham until you reach the river. Cross the bridge and turn left.

Description: Fishes well all year round, but is popular in the winter months with anglers targeting the shoals of roach. Like a lot of rivers in Lincolnshire this section looks and has simular species as many drains in the area. I was lucky and landed some good sized bream and some hungry perch. This stretch is often used for matches and can be busy.

Types of Fish: Bream, roach, perch and pike

Rules/Bans: None

Facilities: Parking behind most pegs.

Telephone: 01652 635224

View from Hibaldstow Bridge

River Glen
Pinchbeck.

Ticket Price: Day ticket £3.50 on the bank.

Directions: From Surfleet to Pinchbeck use the footpath on the south bank. The B1180 runs alongside the south bank of the river between Pinchbeck and West Pinchbeck.

Description: This non-tidal navigation of 11.5 miles begins at Tongue End, near Bourne and passes through several villages before merging with the River Welland at Surfleet Seas End.

Types of Fish: Bream, roach, perch, pike and eel.

Rules/Bans: Not known.

Facilities: Road side parking.

 53

Telephone: 01775 723451 Spalding Fishing Club

River Steeping
Wainfleet.

Ticket Price: Tickets on the bank £3.50.

Directions: Take the A52 from Skegness. Go over the bridge cross the river and turn right, fishing is on this bank only.

Description: This part of the river produces excellent fishing in both the winter and summer months. The perch are a good size and the the roach are in abundance. In the summer the bream and tench can reach over 5lbs.
The downside is that in places this section of river is very shallow at only 2 feet. There are plenty of platforms making access easy for the disabled angler.
Lastly there are some big pike that hunt in the edges. This can be the reason it goes quite for a while.

Types of Fish: Bream, tench, perch, pike, roach.

Rules/Bans: No joker or bloodworm.

Facilities: Parking at the riverside. Disabled access.

Telephone: Skegness Fishing Tackle 01754 611172

River Till
Saxilby, Nr Lincoln.

Ticket Price: Day tickets on the bank £3.50.
Concessions £2.50

Directions: From Lincoln head west towards Saxilby on the A57. After 3 miles the road crosses the river. There is a car park next to the river.

Description: How the river is running decides the method of fishing. If it's flowing use a stick float, but in the summer months it can be very slow and I prefer to use a pole. The River Till is only 20 metres or so in width and looks more like the average drain than a river. Anglers were doing well feeding hemp. Try caster and maggot for the roach and perch.

Types of Fish: Perch, roach, bream, pike.

Rules/Bans: No Bloodworm.

Facilities: Car park near river.

Telephone: 01709 866333 or 01522 534174

River Trent
At North Clifton and Laughterton.

Ticket Price: L&DAA annual memberships are available from local tackle shops.
Adults £25.00. Disabled & OAPs £15.00.
Juniors (under 17) £7.50
Day tickets available at location. £4.00

Description: At North Clifton you can fish the tidal Trent, near the noted "Bridge Peg" that has yielded numerous good catches of chub. The venue holds bream, roach, skimmers, perch, carp and an increasing number of barbel.

Types of Fish: Bream, carp, perch, barbel and roach.

Rules/Bans: No live fish, particle bait, bloodworm & joker.

Contact Details:
J Blades (L&DAA Chairman)
4 Oakleigh Terrace,
Long Leys Road,
Lincoln LN1 1DY
Tel. 01522 560574

Contact Details:
David Ellerker
Secretary
01777 228133

56

Annual Members of the Association can also fish waters of the **Witham & District Joint Anglers Federation** including **Fossdyke Canal** from Brayford Pool to Torksey Lock. **Sincil Drain**, The **River Witham** and a section of the **River Bain** near Coningsby. Also ponds at **Boultham Park**, **Starmers Pit** and **Brewery Farm Lakes**.

Information kindly supplied by
Lincoln & District Angling Association

River Welland
From Spalding to Crowland Bridge.

Ticket Price: Adult: £5.00 per angler.
Junior: (12 or under) £3.00. Senior Citizen: £3.00
Season Ticket Prices: Adult £24.00. Juniors: £5.00
Senior Citizen: £12.00. Juniors are persons aged 12 to 16
years. There is no charge for younger anglers.

Directions: From Peterborough head towards Eye. Take the
A1073 sign posted Crowland. Turn left onto the B1166 and
go through Crowland until you reach the bridge. Peg 1
starts at Spalding and reaches the 700's at Crowland Bridge.

Description: There are bream to double figures, tench to 7lb,
roach average 2lb, carp, chub, pike to double figures and
eels. Waggler, leger or groundbait feeder in the middle or
beyond with red maggot or worm is best. Waggler or pole
method with a maggot on the near shelf is ideal for the small
roach. Eels show in summer months.

Types of Fish: Roach, tench, chub, pike, bream and eel.

Rules/Bans: No bloodworm, joker or live baits.

Facilities: Plenty of parking at the riverside.

Telephone: Peterborough & District AA on 01733 565159

Upper River Witham
From Lincoln to South Hykeham.

Ticket Price: L&DAA annual memberships are available from local tackle shops.
Adults £25.00. Disabled & OAPs £15.00.
Juniors (under 17) £7.00
Day tickets available at location. £4.00

Description: The upper River Witham has a growing reputation for specimen bream. There is also plenty of tench, perch and pike plus the excellent winter roach fishing. There are some platforms for the disabled, between Firth Road and Coulson Road.

Types of Fish: Bream, tench, perch, pike and roach.

Rules/Bans: Do not light fires or discard litter.
No parking on banks at any time.
Bait bans: Live fish, bloodworm, joker, whole tiger nuts.

Contact Details:
J Blades (L&DAA Chairman)
4 Oakleigh Terrace,
Long Leys Road,
Lincoln LN1 1DY
Tel. 01522 560574

Contact Details:
David Ellerker
Secretary
01777 228133

58

Lincolnshire Drains

The area covered is basically between Boston and the Lincolnshire Wolds and takes in waters under the control of Boston & District Angling Association and the Witham & District Joint Angling Federation.

Starting with the **Hobhole Drain**. This runs to the right and parallel with the A16 from just south of the small town of Spilsby to its outfall into the Haven to the east of Boston. This serves all of that eastern area to the coast via smaller (fishable) drains such as the Bellwater and Fodderdyke and even some across to its west side. The water is effectively split into two halfway along its length at the Lade Bank pumping station, above which control is vested in the New Leake AC, and below with the Boston & District A.A. The width ranges from approx 12 metres at its northern end to around 25 metres and more towards the outfall, with depths in the 1.5 – 3 metre category. Most of the water from the top end down to the main road bridge (A52) at Halltoft End has roadside access on the eastern side as well as walking in on the opposite bank

HOBHOLE DRAIN

from the various bridges. Below that there are vehicular accessible tracks on the eastern side between the Clampgate and Nunn's Bridges, right down to the outfall pumping station. Care should be taken in most areas, particularly on the eastern bank where the water is quite some way down from the top of the bank which is also very steep. Taking the water as a whole the drain sports a fair number of bream shoals which include huge specimens to 8lbs. and can give both match and pleasure anglers nets of 50lbs. and much more, as recent NFA national winners can vouch for.

Roach and perch and some hybrids are not in abundance during the summer but are generally in the 4- 8oz. range in the case of the roach, whilst the perch can turn up in any swim, particularly when pleasure fishing, and can be as much as 2lbs. and more.

Whilst feeding into this same drain at Freiston Doors Bridge, the **Cowbridge Drain** in actual fact serves land to the West of the A16 and even the Sibsey Trader Drain and has an unusual feature in that it crosses under that drain at Cowbridge without any direct connection to it. Most of this water is accessed by the north bank from the Bakers to Kelsey bridge, after which it is really only walking from there or the Boston Golf Course. Much the same sort of species, and more in the way of smaller fish, plus a decent head of tench to liven things up during the summer months. Also a couple of bream shoals along this two mile length and seven anglers in a line took weights between 7 and 14KGs in last years national.

Locks at the golf course separate this watercourse from the **West Fen Drain** which serves the whole of the north west area with the Rivers Witham and Bain on its west and north boundaries respectively. In effect the system has a double arm as the Frith Bank Drain which is locked to the Witham at Antons Gowt and

WEST FEN DRAIN

goes around in a wide arc to join up with its sister towards the tiny village of Bunkers Hill. This water is really only fished for the resident bream shoal at the golf course end during the summer months but comes into its own over the winter period in Frithville village where roach nets to 30lbs. or more can be achieved when conditions are favourable.

This brings us to the **Sibsey Trader Drain** system which can be traced from its outfall into the Haven in the middle of Boston right through to the edge of the Wolds to the north some 10 miles hence. Starting from the outfall, the water comes in different guises and from there to Bargate Bridge is known as, logically, the **Bargate Drain** with 70 permanent pegs. The vast majority of these are easily accessed along a footpath with the main parking on Windsor Crescent. This section usually holds a huge population of small roach, perch and skimmers during the summer months together with a fair head of good bream and tench to 5lbs.The other side of the bridge brings you immediately to Maud Foster Mill and so not unnaturally is known as the **Maud Foster Drain** from there to Cowbridge and covers approximately 100 fishable pegs in a drain width of around twenty two metres and depths in the 5 – 6 ft range.

It perhaps contains less in the way of small fish but a bigger head of those bream and tench, which talking of the latter, can turn up in any swim and frequently do. This drain now boasts a good

BARGATE DRAIN

fishing platform at every peg from the outfall at Mount Bridge to a little way short of Cowbridge, around 150 in total. The **Sibsey Trader Drain** itself starts immediately from Cowbridge and continues northwards on the left side of, and parallel to the A16 for some six miles to the village of Sibsey Northlands. Here it splits at Cherry Corner into the East & West Fen Catchwaters, which are in the main unfishable during summer months for too much weed growth and have low water levels during winter (on a normal dry year).

This water is around 20 metres wide, being 5-6 ft in depth and contains a good head of roach, perch, skimmers and large bream but is something of an enigma as small club matches invariably struggle for decent weights on a weekend.

Pleasure fishing and big matches on the other hand usually bring out some super nets of roach, skimmers and those big bream, as can be seen from previous national events.

Roadside access is available from the golf course to Northlands Bridge, around 300 pegs, but currently some sections are out of bounds, due to regulations on overhead power cables, which may be reviewed during this closed season.

SILSEY TRADER DRAIN

The main waterway is the **River Witham** which is much wider and deeper than any other in the area. Also much longer than most realise, starting as it does near S. Witham on the Lincolnshire border with Rutland County. From there it wends its way northwards taking in Grantham and Lincoln before taking a sharp right turn in the city to run down to Boston, some 70 miles or so in total. Not much more than a large delph or beck as it goes from Grantham to Lincoln but certainly in the Long Benington and Claypole area contains many specimen fish of the usual species but also holds many good chub and barbel to spice up proceedings for the pleasure angler. The first named area is controlled by Grantham & DAA whilst the Claypole section comes under Newark & District Piscatorial. Heading into the Lincoln approaches, the water gradually widens and deepens to hold good shoals of roach, perch and bream within the city limits and is administered by Lincoln & District AA. On to the eastern side of the city it now enlarges dramatically to take in the summer boat traffic which uses the waterway to get from the Midlands via the R.Trent and the Fossdyke Canal to access the east coast at Boston. Unfortunately this part of river suffers too much weed in the summer months and is only easily accessible from the various bridges along its 30 mile length. Most of the water comes under the jurisdiction of the Witham & District joint Angling Federation whose jewel in the crown is a small stretch some 4 miles from the Kirkstead to Tattershall bridges through to Chapel Hill, having roadside access. The river is on average 30 or more metres wide and apart from its renowned bream shoals has little else to attract the

pleasure angler as roach and skimmers are too thin on the ground during those summer months. A different story for the winter period as these same fish shoal up in a few pegs at the previously mentioned bridges when water levels are

SOUTH FORTY FOOT DRAIN

well down. Swinging round now to the west and south of Boston, and to the other side of the R. Witham, is another extensive drainage system in the shape of the **South & North Forty Foot Drains**. The South Forty Foot is the main drain which is locked in Boston into the Haven.

This is fed by other much smaller drains including the N. Forty Foot along its entire length, which in total cover a large area of land in a sickle shape going right round to the R. Glen beyond Bourne and to the south of Spalding. Also a little under stocked and suffering from lack of access apart from bridges, nearly all of those smaller drains have pumping stations at their outfall into the main water, effectively preventing any natural fish movement between the two over the course of a year. It does boast some bream but most anglers tackle the venue with roach, perch and skimmers in mind and certainly the Boston end contains its fair share of these during the summer, given that the drain does not suffer salt ingress on a very dry year. Similarly for the N. Forty Foot drain which has good roadside access within Boston as well as around five miles beyond the B1192 towards Holland Fen. Unfortunately this drain, although containing a good variety of fish, does suffer from steep banks and an abundance of summer weed and is hardly a choice for local anglers who tend to choose more amenable facilities – spoilt for choice in other words!

Finally to the south of the county is the Spalding region which also boasts a myriad of drains, many of which are administered by the East Midlands Angling Federation, of which Boston & D.A.A. are a part. The **Coronation Channel** and **Vernatts Drain** are the main waters in and around Spalding town itself. The former is generally at its best during those summer months although access is again limited to bridges. Both waters do contain shoals of bream as well as the occasional tench but also retain an angler's interest with good populations of roach, perch and skimmers. All in all a Boston & D.A.A. book holder has a wealth of waters to go at, and belonging to the other mentioned angling bodies, has access to well over 100 miles of water from the Fossdyke Canal and R. Witham in the north and west, to the Hobhole Drain and Coronation Channel in the east and south.

Ticket Price: Day tickets £3.50. Annual book £20.00. Concessionary annual book £14.00.

Types of Fish: Roach, perch, tench and bream.

Rules/Bans: No bloodworm or joker.

Telephone: To book pegs and match booking ring 01205 871815

Information kindly supplied by Barbara Clifton and Barry Mallett of the Boston & District Angling Association.

T A C K L E   S H O P S
in Lincolnshire

A.J Tackle, 39, Brocklesby Rd, Grimsby, South Humberside DN34 5NF 01472 753090

Boston Angling Centre, 11 Horncastle Rd, Boston, PE21 9BN. 01205 353436

Brigg Angling Centre, Bridge Street, Brigg DN20 8NW. 01652 651650

Castaline, 18-20 Upgate, Louth, Lincolnshire, LN11 9ET. 01507 602149

Castaway Tackle, Unit 8b, Chieftain Way, Tritton Rd Trading Estate, Lincoln, LN6 7RY.
Tel: 01522 567090

Chapmans Angling, 21-27, Beechway, Scunthorpe, DN16 2HF. 01724 862585

Clee Angling, 15 St. Peters Avenue, Cleethorpes, South Humberside DN35 8HQ. 01472 694777

Daves Peg, 33 Westgate, Sleaford, Lincolnshire, NG34 7PU. 01529 415896

Fishing Republic, Unit 5 Ashley Est, Exmoor Ave, Scunthorpe. DN15 8NJ 01724 853232

Ged,s Fenland Tackle, 49 Hallgate, Holbeach, Spalding, PE12 7JA. 01406 422020

Granz Angling, 25 New Rd, Spaulding PE11 1DQ. 01775 712206

Harrisons Tackle, 55 Croft St, Lincoln, Lincolnshire, LN2 5AZ. 01522 523834

Horncastle Pet Centre, 51-53, North St, Horncastle, Lincolnshire LN9 5DX. 01507 523633

Immingham Angling Centre, 381 Pelham Road, Immingham, DN40 1NG. 01469 572358

Oasis Fishing Lakes, Warren Rd, North Somercotes, Louth. LN11 7QX 01507 358488

Oham Lakes, Main Rd, Maltby-le-Marsh, Alford, Lincolnshire, LN13 0JP. 01507 450623

Pauls Tackle, 90 Church Street, Gainsborough, DN21 2JR. 07944 944483

Short Ferry Angling, Ferry Road, Fiskerton, LIncoln LN3 4HU. 01526 399584

Sparks Bros, 43a Cromwell Avenue, Grimsby, N.E. Lincolnshire, DN31 2DR. 01472 342613

Spilsby Angling Centre, 7 Market St, Spilsby, PE23 5JT 01790 755599

Scunthorpe Fishing Tackle Centre, 9 Laneham St, Scunthorpe, Lincolnshire, DN15 6LJ.
Tel: 01724 849815

Storrs, 37-38 High St, Wainfleet, Skegness, PE24 4BJ. 01754 880378

Tackle 4U, 155 Roman Bank, Skegness. PE25 1RY. 01754 611172

The Tackle Shop, Bridge Rd, Gainsborough, Lincolnshire, DN21 1JU. 01427 613002

The Tradin Post, 141 Hainton Avenue, Grimsby, South Humberside DN32 9LF 01472 345376

Ultimate Angling Ltd, 5 Peacefield Business Park, Louth Rd, Holton-le-Clay, Grimsby, DN36 5HS.
Tel: 01472 823777

Used Tackle Superstore, Unit 3, Sea Lane, Ingoldmells, Skegness, Lincolnshire PE25 1PH.
Tel: 01754 872973

Tackle 4U, 2 Midland Buildings, Skegness Rd, Ingoldmells, PE25 1NP. 01754 874950

Whisby Angling Supplies, Unit 6, Exchange Rd, Lincoln, LN6 3JZ. 01522 684464

Windmill Pets & Tackle, 2 High St, Alford. LN13 9DS. 01507 463505

Woodlands Tackle Shop, Ashby Rd, Spilsby, PE23 5DW. 01790 754252

Keep a record of all your fishing trips with

Log-it

Venue:		Address:			Date:
Peg No:	Start Time:		End Time:	Weather Conditions:	

Species	Weight	Method	Rig set up	Ground Bait	Hook Bait	Time

Venue:		Address:			Date:
Peg No:	Start Time:	End Time:	Weather Conditions:		

Species	Weight	Method	Rig set up	Ground Bait	Hook Bait	Time

Venue:		Address:			Date:
Peg No:	Start Time:		End Time:	Weather Conditions:	

Species	Weight	Method	Rig set up	Ground Bait	Hook Bait	Time

F I S H I N G   T E R M S

Here is a list of the words most commonly used. This will help anglers new to the sport to understand fishing terms used by other anglers.

BALE ARM: A revolving arm on a fixed spool reel which winds line onto the spool.

BAGGING UP: A term used when an angler is catching really well, or to describe a venue that is fishing well.

BAIT BANDS: These are small rubber bands. They are aimed at securing difficult to hook baits to the hook. They come in various sizes to accommodate the size of the bait.

BAITING NEEDLE: These pull the hair loop through the bait. They have a mechanism for attaching to the loop whether it is like a small hook, or a pivot that hooks over the loop. The needle is then drawn back through the bait taking the loop and hair with it.

BARBLESS: A type of hook without sharp barbs to help retain bait and fish. Barbed hooks are banned from most fisheries.

BIN LIDS: A slang term for large bream.

BITE ALARMS: These are electronic sensors that detect the movement of line caused by the fish. They usually have an audible alarm or light to alert the angler.

BIVIES: These are domed tents with an opening at the front providing a shelter from the elements.

BOILIES: These are generally hard balls of bait that are primarily designed as a carp bait.

BREAD PUNCH: A bread punch has a circular 'punch' at the end which is pushed down onto a slice of bread and cuts a small piece out which is placed on the hook. There are many different sizes of punches for different hook sizes.

BREAKING STRAIN: The amount of pressure a line will take before snapping.

BUMPED OFF: This term is used by pole anglers, whereby through the use of heavy tactics the fish once hooked is bumped off. This happens when the fish is not big enough to expand the elastic fully.

CASTERS: The chrysalis form of a maggot.

DEADBAITING: The use of dead fish for catching predatory fish such pike, perch, and eels.

DISGORGER: A long device to help remove the hook from a fish's mouth. Always have one with you.

FOUL HOOKED: A fish that has been hooked anywhere else on the body apart from the mouth.

GROUNDBAIT: A dry mixture intended to be thrown into the water to attract fish. Usually consists of bread crumb, crushed biscuit, crushed hemp or other ingredients.

HAIR RIG: A hair rig is generally a piece of line that extends beyond the point of the shank of the hook. On the end of the length of line is a small loop.

HOOKLENGTH: A short length of line, of lesser breaking strength than the mainline, to which the hook is tied. It is used to make it less likely to be detected by the fish. It also ensures that if the line is snapped by a fish, the angler would not then lose the float / swim feeder / leger and all the other shot

Legering: Bait held on the bottom by means of a weight or feeder.

Loosefeed: Small offerings of loose bait, such as maggots or sweetcorn, which are thrown into the water to keep the fish interested in the area you are fishing.

Line bites: False indications of bites usually caused by fish brushing against the line.

Lures: Artificial fish, used to tempt predators such as pike and zander.

Margin: This is an area nearest the bank, that has a shallower depth than that of the main water.

Match fishing: A competitive form of coarse fishing which involves people drawing out a random peg (a place to fish), and then trying to catch as many fish as possible within the allotted time. Usually the winner will be the one with the greatest weight of fish caught.

Peg: A peg is a pre defined fishing area. Venues are split up into evenly spaced fishing zones which are often marked with a wooden peg or marker.

Pinkies: The larvae of the green bottle fly. Small, very lively and great as a loosefeed on stillwaters and canals or as a hookbait for smaller fish.

Plummet: A device used for determining the depth of the water in which you are fishing.

Pole: A pole is constructed from very advanced carbon combinations and comes in various sizes, weight and prices.

Pole rig: These are lengths of line that have the float, weights and a hook attached.

Quiver tip: A special type of rod used to detect bites when ledgering. It has a sensitive tip that curves over when the angler has a bite. Quiver tips vary in strength and stiffness which can be changed according to the weather conditions.

Snags: Features in your swim that are likely to cause you problems They can also be fish holding features such as lilies, overhanging trees, sunken branches. A place to avoid once a fish is hooked.

Spade end hooks: Spade end hooks have an up-turned flattened piece of metal instead of an eye to which to tie the fishing line.

Specimen: A term given to any fish that is a particularly good size for its species.

Strike: To respond to the taking of the bait by pulling the rod in an upwards or sideways motion to hook the fish.

Swim: The area of water where you are fishing.

Tackle: A term used to refer to any fishing equipment (photo tackle)

Test curve: The test curve is the time and weight needed to make the tip bend 90 degrees from the rod butt. Each rod has a test curve with those being used for specimen fish such as carp having a greater test curve than a general coarse rod.

Trotting: Allowing a float to travel at the speed of the current.

Whip: This is a scaled down version of a pole.

I N D E X

If you know of a fishery that is not included in this guide or you want to update an existing venue. Please fill in the form below.

Fishery Name

Fishery Address

Post code

Contact Name

Telephone No

| Adult Day Ticket Price | £ | concession OAP'S | £ |

Fish species and approximate weights

Brief Description

Rules / Bans

Facilities

Number of Lakes

Please e-mail or post a colour photo for inclusion in the next publication.

Please return this form to:
Arc Publishing
166 Knowle Lane,
Bents Green,
Sheffield, S11 9SJ.
Fax: (0114) 2352994

New Fishery ☐

Update to Fishery ☐

New Fishery / Fishery Update Form

Readers Special Offer